FINDING THE SECRET PLACE

THE STORY OF ONE TROUBLED TEEN

FINDING THE SECRET PLACE

THE STORY OF ONE TROUBLED TEEN

LINDA T. STARKS

ISBN 979-8-88526-627-7 paperback
ISBN 979-8-88526-626-0 eBook

DEDICATION

I dedicate this book to the memory of Pete Barton, his precious wife, Mattie, and their children: Zack, Ginger, and Noah.
And to my family, Bo, John, Mattie, and Mark for reaching out to help a troubled teen.

"Yea tho I walk through the valley of the shadow of death, I will fear no evil, for THOU art with me" ... Psalms 23: 4

"And they overcame him by the blood of the Lamb, and by the word of their testimony"...Revelations 12:11

TABLE OF CONTENTS

ACKNOWLEDGEMENT

I want to thank my LORD JESUS CHRIST for life and life more abundantly, for giving me purpose and peace in writing down the thoughts of my heart. I want to thank each one of you who has taken the time to read my book.

I want to thank my dear friend, Lucia Claborn, who has accepted me and has spent countless hours encouraging me to finish this book. She told me Zack should not be incarcerated and that we were going to contend for him. What a wonderful blessing she still is to me.

I want to thank my wonderful cousin, Ron Hamilton, for his relentless positive and encouraging words. Not only did he pray for me, but he also gave me valuable direction for the follow-up of my book.

I want to thank Barbara Hallmark for her dedication to critiquing my book, and especially correcting my punctuation. I was so pleased with her comments.

I want to thank Karin Young for being a stable friend all through my life. We recently celebrated our 50th anniversary and Karin brought a letter that I wrote her when Bo called to ask me to marry him. (He was on his way to Vietnam). Bo had also written Karin after talking to me. They were so funny, and we enjoyed them so much.

And last but not least, I want to thank my awesome husband, Bo, for standing with me all these 50 plus years. His love has carried me through. It has been a journey, and I thank my FATHER it is not over yet.

The first time I saw Pete was in a Tuesday night church service in a small Baptist church in Bastrop, Louisiana. I had heard about him from the kids around town. They said, "He was about the meanest and most respected guy the kids knew." They admired him and his friend, Eric.

This Tuesday night service was not your ordinary church. These were kids who chose not to go to church because "church people thought they were too good to associate with them."

We let them come as they were-long hair, heavy metal tee shirts, holey blue jeans, broken hearts, lonely, sad, abandoned, and lost. We would share JESUS and we prayed with those who would let us. Nothing else would do for them. We did our best to love and accept them.

It was 6:30 p.m. and I found out Pete was home and was at Eric's, so I went to Eric's and begged and pleaded with them to come to church that night. They were listening to their music and tinkering with a car motor.

I thought about Andrew in the Bible. "One of the two that heard John speak was Andrew, Simon Peter's brother, and saith unto him, *'We have found the Messias, which is being interpreted, the Christ.' And he brought him to JESUS.* John 1:40-41. KJV

Eric brought Pete to church that night. He had on a white tee shirt personally designed with his neck and sleeves removed. The heavy metal picture was on the front and a pack of cigarettes was rolled up on one shoulder. His twelve bandanas given to him by friends were tied from his knees to his ankles. What a sight. I thought my heart would burst with joy.

I do not remember what I spoke on, but Pete watched me through his long hair and gave me respect by listening quietly. I knew Eric was so happy. Pete had come home. You see, Pete was incarcerated in a juvenile detention center for alcohol, drugs, theft, and destruction of property. He was home on furlough and was going to be released in two weeks. (This was a trial run that Pete was not aware of.)

What an exciting time it was for Ms. Jane and me. We were leading the group together and she taught most of them in Bastrop High School. We sang, danced, and praised GOD for HIS goodness. We were so drunk on the LORD; we could not seem to stop rejoicing.

Two days later, our bubble burst. Eric, Pete, and his brother were arrested for car theft. Pete was returned to LTI (Louisiana Technical Institute) where he had lived for three years. Eric's dad paid his fine and he did community service. Pete had another year added to his time.

I went to court with Eric and sat in the hall because they were minors. While waiting for the proceedings to begin, they brought Pete into court with chains from his waist to his ankles. I felt like my heart was being ripped out of my chest. GOD had given me such a love for these boys, and I wanted to help them. Jane and I continued to pray for them. We continued with the Tuesday night service for the kids. We enjoyed being with them and prayed with most of them. Everyone in the church was very supportive of us and several of the kids came to church with us.

This is a list of the scriptures GOD gave me to pray for Pete:
1. *"Our God is an awesome God."*
2. *"Love covers a multitude of sins."*
3. *"Mercy triumphs over judgment."*
4. *"If God be for us, who can be against us?"*
5. *"For with God, nothing shall be impossible."*

CHAPTER ONE

What an incredible journey Bo and I have been on for fifty years. This is a small portion of our journey that I want to share with you because Pete Barton's life is worth sharing.

I have always been an analytical person. I would think over things, sometimes for days. I have a vivid imagination and love to search for answers to life's issues. Looking back on my life, I can see GOD'S hand on my life preparing me for this mission I chose. My early years were filled with horseback riding, playing on the bayou, and going to Arkansas to see my grandparents. We were a close family.

I was afraid at night. This is the first time I was aware of the supernatural, but I did not know. When mother would turn out my light, I would see eyes in the room. It was so frightening and the only thing that would dispel them was light. This was a very difficult time in my life. This went on until I became a teenager, then the fear traveled to my mind. I worried about everything. The root of worry is fear. So many things can go through a child's mind, and I was taught to keep it to myself. I buried my fears.

I was raised in a small Southern Baptist church in North Louisiana. I played the piano and sang special music with two friends from church almost every Sunday. Our church invited college students (future pastors) to preach and many of the guys spent the weekend with us. It was exciting to have these visiting young men in our home. They talked about Jesus and studied God's Word. They always talked about saving those that were lost. Several of them would go to the bars on Friday night and witness. This was my junior and senior years in high school and their witness lit a fire for souls in my heart.

My mother taught fifth grade. Because of this, I was exposed to many opportunities to read and learn. From my mother's teaching and example, she encouraged me to read, and I learned to search and explore untold dreams and adventures through books. In other words, I was a dreamer and lived in a fantasy world. LOL. I pretended to live in a hotel. When I went into my room,

I was in my 20s and worked. This enhanced my life because I had no one to play with, so I pretended. I played cowboys and Indians. I also played with dolls. Santa was real until I was 10 years old. I was so upset when an older student told me he was not real. I could not wait to ask my mother. She and Daddy sat me down and told me. Then they said as long as I believed, Santa would come. So, I believed.

Being an only child with older parents, I was with them all the time. They liked me. I was the apple of their eye, so it is not hard to believe the Word of God when it talks about David being the "apple of MY eye." My parents loved me, and I had loving grandparents. I believe my life was enriched by the family in which God put me. I know I felt secure in their love.

Daddy was a farmer, and we rode horses for pleasure. He encouraged me to achieve success in our small riding club. I became the "queen" of our club. I entered the "queen's contest" in local rodeos. You see, I was very shy. I could imagine saying anything, but I was not able to express myself. I knew it in my head; it just did not come out right when I spoke. Today, people laugh when I tell them I have been shy because I love to talk.

We also rode on numerous play days. My cousin, Ron, and I would team together. We fell off a lot during these events. The thing we remember most was laughing. It was so funny, and it brings back special memories even today. It was a wonderful time, and I made several longtime friends. Ron and I have stayed close and enjoyed many phone conversations. We are amazed how we can be away from each other and when calling can see the other on our phone screens.

By the time I was ready to graduate, my goal in life was to become a teacher like my mother. I also wanted 12 children so I would never be alone or miss out on "large family fun." I had never really been away from my parents for more than a night. I was young and naïve.

I started my college journey in 1965, at Louisiana Baptist College in Pineville, Louisiana, majoring in elementary education. Here was this little country girl, going to a Baptist College three hours away from home. I was so excited. My goodness, the transitions I went through from roommates to friends to boosters to learning to become independent. I missed home and my parents very much.

On my first day on campus, mother and daddy left me, 95 miles from home and I did not know anyone. My roommate, Cindy, was very organized, quiet, and stoic. I was very outgoing, loud, and messy.

I found out where I was supposed to be and was preparing to go when I noticed I had a rash. Oh, my goodness! Not just any rash; it was all over my face, neck, and arms. You would have thought I had the measles. I was extremely upset because I was afraid no one would want to be near me. I ran to the infirmary, thank God they had one, and the nurse was very calm. She made me feel so much better. I made it through my first days at school. Joy, oh joy! (The nurse thought it was a nervous rash. It gradually went away.)

The college was small, and I soon made many friends. Our only mode of transportation was walking. It took 25 minutes to get downtown and we thought "Wow!" Now, Cindy was athletic and could outwalk me. She has maintained that characteristic throughout life.

Our campus was small and beautiful with tall trees and shrubs. I had so many good times with my friends and my roommate. Cindy was everything I wanted to be. She was organized, quiet, and never made snap decisions. We enjoyed school. That was one thing we had in common.

One of my friends was Wayne. He lived in Bastrop, which was 20 minutes from my home, and He preached at our little church on weekends. He would call and say,

"We're going home in 15 minutes. I have room for you if you want to go."

"Yes, I will be ready." I would rush to my room, sling together some things, and was on my way home. I did this every time he called, which was almost every weekend.

Cindy reported me when I moved in because I left my boxes all over the room in my haste to leave. Cindy and I have recently renewed our friendship and I mentioned her reporting me. She did not remember turning me in. Knowing Cindy, I think she was just talking with the Dorm Mother (DM) and commented that I left the room in a mess with boxes everywhere. She did not know the DM had written to me. Truthfully, I did not remember it either until cleaning out some papers, I had found the note.

We were so different. Cindy enjoyed reading biographies of well-known people. She liked to read, and I liked to get out and see my friends. I was not interested in reading since I had new territory to explore. Another thing we had in common, we also liked to go to town.

"Linda," she would say, "Let's go to town," or "go join the chorus," or "walk to church," and I was ready to go. Cindy and I did join the chorus on campus. We performed part of the Hallelujah Chorus. It was a nice experience and I enjoyed it very much.

Cindy and I met an elderly lady who owned an old pharmacy downtown. She was lonely, so each time we walked by her store, we would go in and visit. She even invited us home with her. The path to her house was grown up with trees and brush, but we were able to drive to her front door. It was a beautiful home and since her husband had died, she lived there alone. Thinking back, I am sorry we were not able to encourage her more.

One time, I wanted to go home. I had memorized the bus schedules, but for some reason this particular time, in my excitement, I forgot about the schedule. DUH. I found a bus going to Bastrop, Louisiana, leaving at nine p.m. and arriving at one a.m. Cindy went with me, and I was so excited. We took a cab to the bus depot in downtown Alexandria, Louisiana. When we got to our seats and sat down. I was handing the bus driver my ticket.

I said, "Now, when will we get into Bastrop?"

He said, "This bus only goes to Monroe," which is about 35 miles from Bastrop. Mother and Daddy were to meet us in Bastrop at three a.m. I was so upset. I started worrying about the situation we were in, and I could not seem to come up with a solution. I was very verbal with my thoughts. Finally, Cindy says,

"When we get there, (no cell phones at this time), just call the police department and ask them to find your parents in Bastrop. Tell them where we are and to come to get us in Monroe." Then she leaned back in her seat and went to sleep.

That is what I am talking about and why I loved her. Oh, Praise the Lord! So, everything turned out just fine. We had a wonderful weekend, and daddy and mother took us safely back to Louisiana College.

You know, we could get away with things then that I would have never let my children do. I would have been afraid for them to ride a bus, much less at night. (And our ride in a taxi to the bus stop, who would have thought…?)

Cindy had a cousin that she talked about all the time, and I loved to hear about him. One day she said,

"I want you to come home with me and meet my cousin. His name is Bo."

So, I went home with Cindy and met Bo. Oh, my goodness! Oh, my goodness! Bo was my dream mate, my special "knight in shining armor." Lo and behold, he liked me, too. Wow! We started writing and talking on the phone. I never dated so I was not knowledgeable about guys. During the summer months, Bo came to see me almost every weekend either at college or at my home.

Bo has always been "real." If you want his opinion, he will give it to you even if it hurts your feelings. Bo and I often laughed about God putting two different people together to see if we could make it. (So far so good).

Bo stayed in his room most of the school year for making low grades. He somehow was able to obtain a spare report card. (Now, "I wonder how?") LOL. That was the one he showed his parents. During his senior year, he lacked one-half credit graduating so his Daddy made him go the whole year. Since he was only in school for one class, he and his friend became proficient at stealing hubcaps at ballgames. They then moved to stealing cattle. He later told me it was more lucrative. LOL. I want to tell you about these experiences because they were so amazing to me. This is another example of how fearless he is.

Bo lived on 10 acres in the Central Community outside of Baton Rouge. During a football game, he and his friend would sneak out to the parking lot and steal hubcaps. They had quite a stash in the back of his Dad's car. It never occurred to Bo that his Dad would look in the trunk and find the hubcaps, but his dad found them, and he told Bo to get rid of them. He and his friend threw them in the Comite River. Later, they went diving in cold water to try and recover them. He said they were not too successful. LOL.

Since the hubcap venture did not turn out so well, he and his friend decided to steal calves, load them in the friend's truck, and take them to the sale barn. They were very cautious the first time. Every time a dog barked, they would hide. After a seemingly long time, they were successful. The money they made was so much more than the hubcap venture that they continued this for months. God later had Bo make restitution. While in seminary, the LORD convicted him. He went back to the house where they stole the cows and knocked on the door. The previous owners had sold it and a retired missionary couple came to the door. Bo explained why he was there.

They invited him in, and they had a wonderful visit. They would not accept the money. The LORD told him to take it back with him. So, he left home, excited GOD had taken care of it. However, the LORD told him to make an offering of restitution as described in Ezekiel. Well, at the time, we were going to a large church in Memphis while in seminary.

The LORD instructed him to present it there. Bo talked to the pastor, and he told him Bo could present it next Sunday night. Bo was not happy because he was ready to get it over. He did not want to wait. Patience is not one of Bo's virtues. LOL.

That Sunday night he got up and explained what he was doing. When they had an altar call, a man with something in his life for 35 years came forward and repented. Several others came forward. It turned out to be a blessing and a good memory.

I was amazed at Bo's personality. Nothing seemed to bother him as long as things went his way. He handled anger well until he came home from Vietnam, then his anger would get out of control. When I first met him, he was so different from everyone else I knew. I just wanted to be with him. Bo never shared his thoughts with me, and I never knew if he even liked me. Of course, later he told me, "I drove four hours to see you. Was not that good enough?"

Bo Starks' reasoning. Sometimes it was really hard to understand him. LOL. I began to notice little things about him, like not wanting to go to church with me. He was taking me to church one Sunday and suddenly slammed on his brakes. A can of beer spilled all over my wool suit. Now, I worried that everyone would smell beer on me. I had never been around beer before. I was afraid he drank. He told me it was his friends. I was raised to hate alcohol, so this bothered me.

We dated through the summer of 1965. He graduated high school and was living with his aunt in Lake Charles, Louisiana, and working with his uncle. That was about four-five hours from me. He once told me about going with two Lindas. He finally told the other Linda he was breaking up with her. He thought it was funny, HA. I did not.

By October, I had decided to break up with him. He was a loner, and I am a people person.

He really did love me, but he did not express himself any better than I could. So, when he quit his job to come to see me, I broke up with him. I did not know he had to quit his job to come to see me. He then joined the Army for four years. He was extremely compulsive. Why not two years? He left for the Army, and I returned to school. Cindy later told me Bo had joined four years and requested to go to Vietnam.

Cindy and Bo wrote frequently, and she told me, "Bo is in Okinawa, Japan, and he is planning to bring a girl home with him." Well, that got me thinking, "How am I going to feel if I pass Bo walking down the street with his new little girlfriend?" I did not like that thought and could not quit thinking about him. Cindy had his address and I sent him a letter to see where it would lead. Lo, and behold, he answered. Wow! I was excited.

He came home on leave with orders to go to Vietnam. We met at Lake Bruin State Park in Louisiana one weekend. I was worried about not seeing him for so long. How could I talk to him? What would I say? We just started talking. It was good. He was more open, and his family received me graciously. I could not believe my mother let me go camping with his family.

It was a wonderful visit. His childhood friend, Bill was with him. He and his wife, Tammy are special friends to this day. When he left, he called me several days later from San Francisco and asked me to marry him. I was so excited and scared, but I told him "yes." Then I phoned my mother and asked her, "Did I do right?" Later, she told me, "I was not worried because he would be gone a long time and I thought it would never come to anything." HA! Little did she know.

I was so in love with him, and more so 50 plus years later. He is wonderful. Probably because we are so different. We got married in 1968 on his leave. We had a simple wedding in our home with several family members. I found out later the principal would not let Mama miss school, so she was docked her teacher's pay. During the ceremony, Bill dropped a penny and Bo thought he dropped my ring. Our wedding pictures of Bo are hilarious. Some of them resembled a "deer in the headlights."

After a month, Bo finally went back to Vietnam. I just knew he was in trouble since he had stayed longer than his leave, but they did not do anything to him. Bo had an interesting life in Vietnam, being a military policeman (MP in the Army). He was a teenager with a gun, in a hostile country and a military that was underdeveloped.

Bo served 28 months in Vietnam, and he was discharged home in August 1969. And, Oh Dear Lord! I thought I was so ready to have my sweet, loving, courteous husband home. He always walked me to the door and opened the car door for me.

I was not prepared for the Bo that came home. He was hyper, easily excited, and opinionated, not to mention becoming angry about most everything. We had some loud confrontations.

I finally finished college in Monroe, Louisiana, with a bachelor's degree in nursing. Do not even ask me how that came about! I know it was from the Lord. My major was elementary education. If I knew then what I know now, I would have gotten a double degree.

Bo got a degree in general studies and graduated in 1973. He had started a history major, but his foreign language was Russian. Sometime during the four years, the teacher left, and he then changed majors to general studies.

I did not know a lot about answered prayers. I read and studied the Bible, memorizing many verses, but I did not have a prayer life. I just loved JESUS. I remember going down front one Sunday morning when I was seven and accepted JESUS as my Savior. Later, I started having doubts about my salvation because one of our pastors commented, "If you did not know you were lost, you did not get saved." I doubted my salvation for years.

Now, years later, my church, Cornerstone Christian Fellowship, prays out loud every Sunday with people that want to be saved. This has helped me tremendously to have faith to know I am saved.

CHAPTER TWO

Bill and his wife moved to North Louisiana. He and Bo decided to build a pen in the back of the field to catch a wild sow and little pigs. They asked a dear neighbor how to build a pen. He told them and they built a pen and scattered corn over the ground. They were able to catch the sow and pigs so then they decided to rope the sow.

I do not know what they were going to do with her, but they finally got a rope around her neck and drove from the back of the field to the front. It was a short distance but when they got to our house, they had strangled the sow. Bo and Bill just stood there looking at her for the longest time, then they called the neighbor and told him what had happened. They took a lot of "ribbing" from our friends. They cleaned and cut up the sow. It was not the best meat I had ever eaten.

Fast forward to 1973. After several miscarriages, we had our first child, a little boy in February. We named him John. He won my heart immediately, but he had colic and cried a lot. I was in school during this time, and I learned the stages of emotional growth. John did not fit any stage. He cried about 24 hours a day. Our neighbor would visit, and she would put him on her lap. He would promptly fall asleep. I loved him so much. I took him everywhere I went outside of work. He eventually outgrew the colic and became a happy baby. I enjoyed putting him in a grocery cart and playing with him as we shopped. He would laugh, then I would laugh. He was so precious.

I began to notice little things about our home. It was not peaceful like my home had been, growing up. At home, we did not yell, and mother and daddy spoke in a normal voice. We went to church a lot.

There was a lot of yelling and discord in my new home. We are very passionate people, and Bo and I felt we needed to express ourselves to each other, regardless of how it sounded to others. Some people might call it "getting the last word." LOL.

Our conversations were a tool used to get a point across on any subject. It sounds like arguing and it was about everything. I thought it was fun because I had never had anyone to stand up to me and undoubtedly, Bo had not either. I can truthfully say that for 49 years we have continued this habit. In October 2017, God convicted me of strife. Trying to break a 49-year habit is hard. LOL.

During his first years after Vietnam, we had no goals or limits on our actions. I will mention a couple of our experiences. Once, we were getting ready to go out and Bo was bathing. He called me to bring him a new bar of soap. I was drying my hair, which was very long. He yelled again, and again, so I got the soap and hurled it into the bathroom, missing him, of course. LOL. His reaction was not what I expected. I heard him getting out of the bathtub, so I flew out of the house to get away from him. That did not bother Bo. He jumped out of the bathtub and chased me down our country road. There was no traffic, but I had lived there all my life and I was not interested in anyone seeing us, so I stopped running. We were laughing so hard as we went back into the house, and he never did fuss at me.

Another time, I remember, Bo was trying to fix a flat tire. He was always loud and verbal, so I was looking out the window to see what was going on. He was on his knees, and he leaned back and just stared ahead, looking like he was deep in thought. Then he got up, went into the kitchen, got the teakettle off the stove, and went back outside. As soon as he stepped off the last step, he drew back and slammed the teakettle down on the concrete. Of course, it broke the teakettle, and all this time, I am still watching. Then he grabbed the jack and threw it as hard as he could. It sailed across the road into the cotton field. I never did know what that was all about. I was learning not to confront him. I laughed and laughed at the expression on his face. It surely was funny.

Spiritually, we had a visiting preacher come to Tillou. This was the first time I had ever met anyone that prayed, and his prayers were answered. It was awesome and I hung on to his every word. He taught us about GOD's enemy. I began to realize why our home had so much turmoil. I was also dealing with increasing fear. Especially if Bo was late from work, I started imagining him lying on the side of the road dying. This evangelist helped me pray through this and bring me peace. I was getting free, and Bo thought I was needing a psychiatrist. LOL. I was not working during this time, and I studied and prayed for hours. This started a new level of understanding about GOD's way that has grown through the years. I learned about and practiced "Deliverance," which is moving enemy forces out of a person's life. What a wonderful thing to discover. GOD is so good.

Fast forward to 1975. We had a beautiful little girl in March, Mattie. Her personality was opposite of John's. John was laid back, photogenic, and played quietly, as long as he was close to me. Mattie was adventurous and loved to climb. She just needed to check on me once in a while to be sure I was still around. I had to keep an eye on Mattie most of the time to be sure she was not in danger. I pulled her off the top of the cabinet many times. She would climb up and open the cabinet door then continue climbing making it to the ceiling. With my heart in my throat, I would climb up and pull her down. She laughed a lot and was such a joy. John and Mattie played well together. We lived on the farm in a rental house, and they loved to go to my parents. Mother had retired from teaching and enjoyed her grandchildren. She was a wonderful mother.

As John grew older, he played with the neighbor's boys. They rode horses, built forts, and did other things boys in the country do. Although Mattie spent time with the boys, she also played with dolls. She would line them all up and teach them, often whipping one for bad behavior. LOL. She was delightful. I would take them both to town, but we could not play as easily because John had to walk beside the cart. They were both well behaved. I was so proud of them. Back then, we dressed our children to go to town, so they always looked sweet. I also took them to a restaurant and taught them how to act. They did so well. I loved this time in my life.

Fast forward again to 1978. We completed our family with another little boy. His name is Mark. Mattie thought he was her baby. She would put him on her hip after he got older and carry him everywhere. He was a joy. He laughed and played with Mattie until he got older, then became John's shadow.

We lived on the farm and attended Tillou Baptist Church outside Bastrop, Louisiana. Daddy and mother were living at the Chemin-A-Haut state park during this time. We owned 102 acres with a farmhouse and a rental house on our property. Our neighbors also had an addition to their family when we had Mark. She and Mark were as close as brother and sister. She always went with us to see my grandparents. Mother and I would help them pick and put up their garden. Grandpa also raised tomatoes for sale and mother and daddy helped him with loading and taking them to market. My uncles also came and helped.

Years passed, and they were filled with church, school, work, and camping. Bo entertained us with stories and witty sayings. On one camping trip, we were with friends in Hot Springs, Arkansas. We were eating lunch near a beautiful stream and the children were off playing. Bo picked up one of the red delicious apples off the table and said, "Do you think I can put this apple in my mouth and shut my mouth?"

Of course, the guys said, "NO! We do not think you can!"

Bo then proceeded to insert the apple in his mouth. Some of us were on the ground laughing and some doubled over on the benches laughing. Bo finally got the apple in his mouth and shut his mouth. By this time, we were almost hysterical, laughing. Then, he tried to get the apple out. Apple bits were flying everywhere. The longer he worked, the funnier it got. When he finally cleaned his mouth, all he said was,

"I told you I could do it." Y'all would have let me die. I could not breathe!" This memory stands out in our life as one of our best. LOL.

Bo was called to preach in 1983 and decided to go to seminary in Memphis, Tennessee. What a transition. We moved in a small subdivision and our kids stayed outside with all the other kids on our street. They learned a lot of things I was not ready for them to know. For example, we still whipped our kids for disobedience. The other kids told them they could get help by calling 1-800-child-abuse. Well, John got in trouble, and I called him into the bathroom for correction. As I began to whip him, he turns around and says,

"I am going to call 1-800-child-abuse on you." I was so shocked! I turned the plastic fly swatter around and hit him three times with the other end and then said,

"Well, now you have something to show them."

I think we both grew with this experience. He was 12 years old and he never smart-mouthed me again. I never whipped him again. When he was little, I timed him out one to three minutes. He just needed to calm down. So, as he got older, about every month he would smart off, thus the whippings.

While Bo was in seminary, we went camping. All we had to sleep in was a zippered room. I carried an electric blanket, so we were comfortable. About 11:00 p.m. Bo whispered in my ear to look at the skunk right beside our screen room. We watched a while, then quietly woke the kids. We watched that skunk until it left. It was great. I thought I had the best little family in the world. They are wonderful. I am very proud of them.

Bo graduated from seminary in 1985 and we moved back to the farm. Many of the good memories the kids have are of learning to live in a subdivision, walking to the ice cream store, and getting ice cream. Then they walked home while eating their treat. I cooked many meals and found out later it was not eaten because they ate ice cream. LOL

After moving home, Bo went to a school in Baton Rouge, Louisiana, for a certificate in electrical instrumentation and was educated to work in a plant. He was still preaching and was pastor of a small Baptist church outside Bastrop, Louisiana. When he graduated, he took a job in Camden, Arkansas, and we moved. Mark stayed with his grandmother in Fountain Hill, Arkansas, and John and Mattie went to school at Fairview High School. John joined the football team, and he practiced every afternoon. Mattie and Pete visited with each other, and Mark was in Fountain Hill with Mamaw Tilbury.

We would go to school and watch John play football. He was a dedicated young man. He still had a girlfriend in Louisiana, and at some point, she came up and John asked her to marry him on the football field. She said yes.

The following begins our story with Pete.

CHAPTER THREE

PETE.

My name is Pete, and I am eight years old. My best friend is Eric. He lived two doors down from my house and we had a good time going around the neighborhood laughing and playing, just being little boys. We went to school within walking distance. I did not like school, and I was not interested in learning. I began to get in trouble at school because I liked to fight. My teachers were patient with me, but sometimes I pushed them to the limit. "Some might even say I am hardheaded. I just figure if I know something, I know something."

When we were 12 years old, we started stealing bicycles and I became quite good at trick riding. We also worked on our "borrowed" bikes to keep them moving. No one ever caught us I had two brothers and one sister. I was the middle child. Mama said I was quiet and liked to help her in the garden and clean the house. She was a nursing assistant, and my dad was a mechanic. There were always several customers' cars in the yard.

My home was always filled with friends. It felt like a party every night. My dad would sit in the kitchen and drink beer, and he stacked the cans up on the table. When he had enough, he would slip off to bed. I did not have much of a relationship with my dad, although I was close to my mom.

Every Christmas, we went to my maternal grandparents with all the other cousins. We opened presents and ate homemade biscuits with tomato gravy. I enjoyed this very much. By the time we were 13 years old, Eric and I started experimenting with mushrooms. We would boil the mushrooms and drink the juice to get high. We were still stealing bicycles and getting high on boiled mushrooms. We had also discovered marijuana and were smoking it.

We were still in school, but like I said, "I liked to fight." Many times, teachers had to take me to the office and call my parents. I just ignored it all. I thought I was happy with my life. As time went by, we decided we needed to have tattoos like our favorite heavy metal group. We rigged up a tattoo gun and started putting tattoos on us and all our friends.

We finally got caught stealing bikes but with only a warning, we were let go. When I was 14 years old, I was high, and I stole one of the cars left for my dad to work on. I drove it down the road and crashed into a light pole. When the police came, my dad said,

"I cannot do anything with him. Take him with you."

I was taken to the city jail in Bastrop, Louisiana. I went to court and was sentenced to two years' incarceration in Louisiana Technical Institute for Juveniles (LTI) in Monroe, Louisiana. As I said, "I liked to fight. It relieved a lot of tension. I became known as 'the fighter.' They would bring other inmates from other prisons to fight me. When I got tired of being in the general population, I would start a fight with an inmate, and they would put me in lockdown. That way, I did not have to deal with anyone or anything."

"When I was first locked up, I prayed and prayed for God to get me out. When HE did not let me out, I gave up believing. I still prayed at times that God would get me out. Little did I know what God had planned for me. It would change my life forever.

My mother always loaded up her car and came to see me most every Sunday. It was about 50 miles from home. She always brought a girlfriend. Ms. Linda tried to come with her one time, but she told her she did not have room.

Days passed.

CHAPTER FOUR

LINDA.

I had a sweet friend named Jane. She was an Algebra teacher, and I was an R.N. Our husbands were pastors, and our children went to private school together. As our children visited, Jane and I spent a long time together talking about the Lord. She talked a lot about her students. They were in a public school, and many were from homes with dysfunctional families. Because of our personalities, we feel things deeply and Jane wanted to see her students serving the Lord. Most of them were not in church.

Every week we prayed for her students. After several months, we decided to start a class for these students. We talked to Bo, and he talked to the people in our church about starting a teenage class on Tuesday night, and our church agreed to let us meet in church. We were so excited. We planned out our program and how we would present Jesus to the students.

No one came the first Tuesday night. Jane had told them they could come however they were dressed, and we expected at least one person. The next Tuesday night, we went to Eric's home since

Jane had expressed a desire to see him saved. He told us he could not come, but his grandmother told us he could come. Our kids pulled him in the car with us, and we went to church that night and talked about the Lord.

Our girls were fascinated with him. His hair was shoulder length and curly. His eyes were blue-green and when he smiled, they sparkled. He was so cute. LOL. He wore heavy metal tee shirts with the arms and neck torn out. He wore blue jeans with doo rags tied from his knees to his ankles. His friends had given him the handkerchiefs. If he had worn a band around his hair, he would have looked like an Indian. It was very colorful and actually, was the way heavy metal groups dressed.

Other students began to come, and a lot of Eric's friends came. After a time, more and more kids started coming. We tried to only meet for an hour, and we had many students and people come, but seldom at the same time. We did not keep up with the number who came or everyone we prayed with. Most of them were in school.

Eric always came with a beautiful girl on his arm. He was quiet, considerate, and smiled a lot and we all enjoyed being around him. Since it was our goal to lead Eric to the Lord, we were so excited when he came back the second week of school and told us he had gone to church with his aunt and had gotten saved. When he told Jane and me, we jumped up and down and praised the Lord.

Eric spent the weekends in our home and went to church with us. Bo and the kids played football, kickball, and hide and go seek at night. They had a good time. We had two roosters that learned to play kickball. It was funny to watch Bo and the kids play kickball with the two roosters.

We were living in Rayville, Louisiana. Bo was laying bricks and I was a nurse in another small town. Bo was still preaching at the church outside Bastrop at this time and our kids were in private school. It seemed like we were happy.

Back to the Tuesday night class. One young girl came to Sunday church with us. When Bo got up to preach, she would turn around with her back to him. When she turned back around, she would stick out her tongue. It always shocked him because he is single-minded, and it would throw him off what he was saying. LOL. She had black fingernails before they were popular. She also cut her arms and the kids told me she practiced witchcraft. I was just glad she made the effort to come to church on Sunday.

We saw this young lady many years later, and she was glad to see us. She had a good job and a baby. It was good to see her and know we had touched her life. God says, "His Word will not come back void without accomplishing what pleases Him."

Eric's mother had left him and his brother when they were small, and they lived with his dad and maternal grandmother. His aunt also took him to church when he did not go with us. Eric wanted to start a rock band and he can play the guitar very well, but it was heavy metal music. One special band was his main group. LOL. He wanted me to listen to his group because he loved his music. At first, I said, "no," but he kept at me until I told him I would listen just to see what he liked about him.

I did learn to listen to certain songs. Their music ministers to the soul. Since I am prone to depression, I realized I needed to stop listening. It was a learning experience for me and caused our children to start listening to metal. I was not happy with that, and John still listens. The only exposure to music our children had before this was Christian music.

There was another young man that I grew close to that I carried to class. He lived with his grandmother and went to church with her. He was a bright young man with many issues including an alternate lifestyle. I found out later that he had committed suicide. God says, "NOTHING will snatch them out of My Hand." Thank you, Lord, that he knew YOU.

Pete was incarcerated for alcohol, drugs, and theft-repeat offender. Jane's dad worked for LTI, and he was able to get us into a class with Pete included. I have learned that when God is in charge, everything just falls into place.

Pete came to class, and I got my second look at him. I was so excited. His hair was to his collar and his bangs were below his eyes. He had to shake it out of his eyes to see. He made eye contact with me, and we stared for a moment. I was so pleased and looked forward to what God had in store for us. We only met that one time, but God put him in my heart as he did for Eric.

We were already praying for Pete at church. Eric would remind us of that when Bo asked for prayer. I can still see Bo many times on his knees in the front pew at church, praying for Pete. His prayer was "Lord, please raise up someone to help Pete."

In July 1989, Bo had stopped preaching and accepted a job in Camden, Arkansas, working in industrial construction. He had recently graduated from International Technical Institute (ITI) as an industrial electrician.

CHAPTER FIVE

PETE.

Today, July 4, 1989, the day started like any other day. I had been in LTI for three years because every time they would give me leave I would get into trouble again. I was bored. A guard had come to work in the evenings and was sitting around with me and two other inmates. The guard was mad because he had dropped his bottle of whiskey and broken it. He had brought it to celebrate the 4th.

We asked him, "Hey man, why don't you let us go?"

He thought a second and then said, "All right, I will let you go out the back gate and I will give you 30 minutes before I call the alarm."

We ran onto the funeral home parking lot behind LTI. We jumped into a hearse and tried to jump it off. About this time, a police car cruising around turned into the parking lot. I jumped out and slipped into the bushes and hid. The other two inmates were captured, but I was able to slip away. I headed home to Bastrop, Louisiana, by following a railroad track. I was not concerned about getting caught at home. I just took it as it came, no worries. (That was Pete)

I called Eric and told him I was home. He came over and we were talking. Now Eric looked out for me. He worried about me. After visiting a while, I told Eric I thought I would go to St. Louis to deal drugs

. Eric said, "You do not want to do that and just looked at me."

He told me about Ms. Linda and the Starks clan. He talked to me for quite a while and convinced me they could help me. It did not matter to me. How bad could it be? At least I would not go back to jail.

I told him, "Go ahead and call them. I will go with them." I waited while Eric called. After a while, they called him back,

"Yes, they would come and get me." Eric seemed happy about this. I would just wait and see.

LINDA.

We were staying at the farm and after Bo graduated from ITI, he took a job in Camden, Arkansas. We were leaving the next day. Bo was outside and I was in the house when I got a call from Eric telling me Pete had escaped LTI and was home. Then he said,

"He says he'll go with you."

I said, "What!"

Eric said, "Pete said he would go with you to Arkansas."

At first, I was shocked. I could not believe he agreed to go with us. I figured when we got to his house, he would change his mind.

I told Eric I had to ask Bo. I went out front by the cars and told Bo what Eric had told me about Pete.

He said, "What do you want me to do?"

I said, "I want you to let me go get him at his house."

Bo stood there a minute, then said, "Well, go and get him."

It was dusky dark, and we were leaving early the next morning. I remembered many Sunday nights at church, Bo getting on his knees and imploring God to raise up someone to help Pete. I told Pete later that the reason God did not answer his prayers about getting out of jail was that God had to prepare someone to help him The Starks Clan.

PETE.

All three of their children wanted to come with Ms. Linda, so they got in their little car and came to my house. Eric was there and met Ms. Linda at the door. The lights were dim, and the house was smoky, but that is how it always was. I was on my knees, working on a stereo. My back was to her, and I never turned around.

Eric said, "This is Ms. Linda."

She said, "Hi, Pete, Eric says you will come with us. We are going back to Arkansas tomorrow. Will you go with us?"

I kept my back to her, but said, "Yes."

I told Eric bye and we went out and got in their car. Her children had been patient and remained in the car. When we got into the car, they covered me up so no one could see me. I was very accommodating. LOL.

Mattie leaned up from the back seat and whispered, "Mama, he needs clothes. He has on girl's pants."

I did not hear this conversation, but she said, "We'll get him some new ones."

She could not believe I had agreed to go with them. Ms. Linda was trying to hear God and she was very afraid. She did not have a game plan, other than bringing me home, getting me safe, and leading me to the Lord. Of course, I did not know any of this.

The next morning, we left for Camden, Arkansas, which was about three hours, and the car was filled with family noises. We got to Camden and found a nice brick house in a nice subdivision. I was going to stay with John in his room. Mattie had a room and Mark was at Mamaw Tilbury's going to school there. The next day Ms. Linda took John and Mattie to school and registered them in class, and I spent my day riding around on a bike. Mr. Bo had gone to work, but I could not work because I would fail the drug test.

CHAPTER SIX

LINDA.

While staying with us, Pete would make the kids French fries, potted meat sandwiches, and ketchup sandwiches. They had never eaten these kinds of sandwiches and they thought they were great. Pete also cleaned and washed clothes. Then Bo finally took him aside and told him we did not get him to be our maid. Pete just looked at him. LOL.

We lived in a nice subdivision in Camden, Arkansas. The public school our children were attending was good and John wanted to play football, so he practiced most evenings through the week with ball games on weekends. I had continued to work in Louisiana, so I left every Sunday night and came home on Friday. I found out later that Pete was checking Mattie out of school early so he could visit with her. They would then go back to school to get the boys. From what I found out later, Pete was picking her up frequently. Bo wanted to get him a job, but he would have failed the drug test, so we had to wait.

When Jane and I had taught the class, we never worried about these boys fooling around with our daughters. She had three girls and I had one. For this reason, I never worried about Mattie and Pete. Pete spent a lot of time talking to the boys and Mattie. He was quiet, pleasant, and our only problem with him was he smoked like a freight train. LOL. During this time, smoking was not considered dangerous, so we let him smoke in the house.

Our ritual was to go to bed around nine o'clock, sleep all night, then get up and start our day. The first night Pete was with us, Bo woke me up at two a.m. and grabbed me exclaiming, "OUR HOUSE IS ON FIRE!" We soon discovered our house was not on fire, but Pete was smoking. He also had to listen to the radio all night, and this bothered John. However, John never complained.

John was playing football so we would go to his games and watch him play football every weekend. The football team wanted to date Mattie, but she only had eyes for Pete, his long hair, and 27 tattoos.

PETE.

I started going with Ms. Linda to my parent's home back in Bastrop, Louisiana. Ms. Linda did not like this but felt if she said anything to me, it would infringe on my rights. She told me later, she did not know me very well then, but she did not like taking me home.

At first, we talked a lot on the way home. It was about two hours. We talked about all kinds of things, but soon Ms. Linda noticed I would get in the car and go straight to sleep. It did not take her long to realize I was high. She just kept praying for me.

In October, I had been with them for three months. Halloween night, Ms. Linda had to work in Louisiana. Bo and the kids decided to get candy for trick or treat. They turned the outside light on and took turns wearing a mask to scare the kids coming to trick or treat. They ran out of candy and had to run to the store several times to get more candy. We found out later that our subdivision was a big draw for the entire town and parents would drive up a block and let their children out to go to every house on the block. Bo and the kids had a really good time.

Bo let one kid come into the house to use the bathroom and when he came to go back out, their mask scared him, and his mask scared them. It was so funny they laughed for a long time. They scared many children that night with their masks. Ms. Linda and I were in Louisiana, so we missed this excitement. Ms. Linda was upset because they were not supposed to celebrate Halloween. She was shocked Bo had done that. LOL.

When I could pass the drug test, I went to work with Bo. I enjoyed work and never missed a day. I think I got good at work. Bo would praise me, and I liked that. While I was waiting to let drugs get out of my system, I had stopped going home with Ms. Linda back to Bastrop. Mattie and I spent every free moment together and talked endlessly. They let us use their car to ride around town.

Sometime in November, God told Ms. Linda that Mattie and I were intimate. She told Bo to talk to us and I just lied. "Who cared if I lied? No one, right? Wrong!" Bo told Ms. Linda he had sat us down and talked to us and we had assured him we were innocent. To him, that was enough, but not to Ms. Linda. She worried about it all week and when she came home Friday night, she approached Bo and told him we were together. He said, "You just will not let it go, will you?!"

Ms. Linda said, "Call Pete in here and ask him and let Mattie stay in her bedroom." I looked Bo straight in the eye and said, "No sir, we're not."

Bo looked at Ms. Linda and said, "Are you happy now?" She said, "Pete, you're telling me you're innocent of this accusation about our daughter and you," and I lied again, "Yes ma'am, we're innocent

Bo then said, "You just will not let it go, will you?"

Ms. Linda said, "Ok, but you are going to pray and let it fall on your head, and I will shut up."

So, Bo prayed with me and Ms. Linda. I went back into Mattie's room and told her what was said. She did not have much to say. Ms. Linda believed what GOD had told her. Since Ms. Linda was an R.N., she observed Mattie closely. She soon realized Mattie was pregnant and took her to the doctor. Our job was ending, and Mattie was pregnant. I realized I loved her, and we were very excited about our baby. I wanted to marry Mattie and we went to town to look at rings. The next day we were riding around, and I put the ring box in her lap. She said, "What is this?"

She opened the box and found a pretty solitaire that she had picked out. I just looked at her, and she said, "Yes." We then went home and shared the news with Bo and Ms. Linda. Bo told Mattie she did not have to marry me and that they would help her and the baby.

Mattie said, "If you do not let us get married, I will leave with him." She was 14 years old. This was not an option for Ms. Linda!

I had asked Mattie to marry me, a fugitive. I did not look or dress like them. I listened to heavy metal music and smoked in the house. I woke up around one or two and smoked. I found out later that Bo and Ms. Linda would dress warmly and walk briskly around our subdivision. Ms. Linda told me they did not talk. There was nothing to say. Mattie and I were so excited, and her parents were speechless.

Ms. Linda planned a wedding in two weeks. She had trouble finding a church and someone told her about a community center. It was a little block building and she decorated it for the wedding. Bo married us. I picked out a song for Mattie and they played it. The song was by Kiss, *"I Was Made For You."* Bo's stepmother wore a mink coat, and my brother wore sunglasses because he had recently been in a fight. Mother had asked one time, "How did I stand living with them, she could not do it."

Mattie's aunts, Aunt Fanny, and Aunt Barbara brought Mattie a wedding dress and all the food. Mattie looked really beautiful. Her family sat on one side and mine sat on the other. I think the only visitors were Bo and Linda's friends from Bastrop. After the reception, Mattie and I went to spend the night at the Holiday Inn. I asked if we needed to bring sheets and she said No. I did not know. My stay in motels was different. The next day, we packed up and went to Louisiana to Mattie's grandparents for Christmas.

CHAPTER SEVEN

LINDA.

On January 4, 1990, we left Louisiana for Greenville, North Carolina. I was so naive, that I packed two blankets, four pillows, two comforters, sheets, a large skillet, and our clothes. I thought God would just point us straight to a place to stay. We tried to travel in a caravan with two of Bo's work buddies, but one couple did not stay with us. It was not a pleasant trip. We left Mark in Hamburg, Arkansas, with my sweet mother, and John in Rayville, Louisiana, with his girlfriend's family.

When we got to Greenville, the couple that did not stay with us on the trip, suddenly found us. We helped her find a place after driving her around for several days. By the time that was over, we only had enough money for two more nights at the motel. We got the paper and searched and searched.

Bo was at work and Pete, Mattie, and I were looking for a place to stay. We found several places, but when they realized Pete and Mattie were not brother and sister, they wanted double rent.

I was so frustrated. I was also afraid someone would see Pete and arrest him. My anxiety level was high. I was doing my best to trust God. I had always taught my children to look at situations as either depression or an adventure. My adventure had changed into a depression. I remember, we decided to eat at KFC. I was crying, Mattie was crying.

I said, "If we do not find something today, I am going back home."

Pete listened to us, then in his laid-back self, calmly said,

"I wish I was still in jail."

Mattie and I looked at him in shock and burst into laughter. Needless to say, that lifted our moods tremendously. I called a man who rented trailers. I had never stayed in one, but so what, I would give it a try. This man did not have anything to rent, but he knew a man that also rented trailers. He gave me his name and number. It was already five p.m. when we called this man and he said he had one trailer for rent. He gave us directions and we happily made the short trip to his trailer park. Our trailer was last in the park, but we did not care. We were so excited. This two-bedroom, one-bath trailer had a $200.00 deposit, and we could pay the rest Friday when Bo got paid. Yea!

I told him Pete and Mattie were married and he said that was ok. As we went into the trailer, I noticed a large barrel turned sideways on stilts.

"What is that?" I asked.

The man said, "Oh, that is for the kerosene. That is what we use for heat."

He gave me a phone number to call for kerosene. There was no widespread use of cell phones, so we were really on our own. I could not wait for Bo to get there. We had a place to stay. Joy, oh joy!

Since this was our second adventure "traveling construction," we went from a three-bedroom brick home in a nice neighborhood to a two-bedroom trailer with kerosene for heat. We were so excited to finally find something. The inside of the trailer looked like it came from a third-world country. We could not afford to buy kerosene and electricity, so we voted for electricity.

The next day, Pete and Mattie scrubbed their entire bedroom walls with Clorox. We wore our shoes when we walked around inside on the carpet. I put a sheet over the couch, and I washed the walls in the living room. We "NEVER" used the oven because it looked like someone cooked a live cat. My stress level was so high with everything, and I just did not think I could clean it.

We had a crockpot that we heated water for coffee, and we bought take-out for our supper. It was so cold. There were no blinds, and the curtains were a thin floral print. Bo and I slept in our clothes, with our sheet, and our one blanket. We snuggled close. LOL. We found one birthday candle and put it on the kitchen table. Bo changed the dryer to blow in the bathroom, so we went in there to get warm, and took turns getting dressed. Is this still an adventure!? LOL.

Pete could not work till he was clean of drugs, so while they slept, I drove Bo to work so we could keep the car. As I said, it was a stressful time for me. I continued to pray. I had no peace but continued to make plans.

After living in this trailer for several weeks, the owner told me he had a three-bedroom trailer, and we could have it if we wanted it. We did! This trailer was clean and close to the main entrance. The only problem was a huge rat we could not catch. We named it "Rosco." LOL. It was the best of times and the worst of times. God was with us, and things began to come together. I was still very stressed.

I went to get Mark in Arkansas and later, Laney came and drove my parents' camper with them. John and Laney wanted to get married so we planned a wedding for John and Laney. We were going to a Methodist church at that time. It was a beautiful wedding and they seemed so happy. John wore a top hat and carried a cane. Laney looked beautiful in her white dress.

After getting everything settled, we found an OB-GYN for Mattie and discovered North Carolina provided for teenage pregnancy. It was a blessing to have a good doctor. While I worked there, I was impressed how well private doctors and doctors from the school of medicine got along so well. Pitt Memorial Hospital was a good place to work. I enjoyed it and met some special ladies.

Mattie and I went shopping for baby things. We found a bassinet and several blankets and towels. Mattie wanted to buy little girl outfits, but I encouraged her to wait until the ultrasound. When she had the ultrasound, she found out it was a little boy. She never mentioned having a little girl again. There was an air of excitement around our trailer. I was excited about the baby and working kept my mind off all the other issues I was handling. Still praying and holding on to JESUS' hand.

Later, we found a wonderful couple who owned two trailers and an old farmhouse for rent. It was a wonderful place. John and Laney moved into the farmhouse, Pete and Mattie moved in one trailer and we moved in the other one. Mark was 12 years old and had come to live with us. He became friends with the farmer there and learned about growing tobacco. He got a job with the man and enjoyed it very much. I was so proud of him. I began to relax a little and enjoy just being alive.

I was working full-time at Pitt Memorial Hospital in Labor and Delivery. We put Mark in a private school. By Christmas, he was way behind. He wanted to go back to Mamaw's and go to school in Fountain Hill so we let him. He went to summer school to catch up and played basketball that fall. I loved watching him play and he could hear me screaming for him on the court. LOL.

Pete finally went to work with Bo. They worked 12-hour days. John was working at a chicken restaurant. He accidentally dropped his lighter in the hot grease and got burned. He had to go to the ER, but everything turned out ok.

Mattie stayed home. She gained a large amount of weight, and the doctor was concerned. We found out later the reason she was gaining so much weight was that she was drinking a liter of coke a day while watching soap operas. My goodness! My precious teenager.

Pete and Mattie took a parenting class to include preparation for labor and delivery. Her doctor scheduled her induction on July 31, at seven a.m. I was at work when she and Pete came in and they were placed in a room. My supervisor would not let me labor Mattie, so I would run in and out checking on her. When I got off at 3:00, the nurse told me she was going to have a caesarian section because she had stopped dilating. They did let Pete and me go into the surgery suite. Pete was in a green scrub suit, and I was so excited.

Zack was so big, they had to use forceps to get him out. He weighed 9lbs and 10 ounces. They named him Pete and called him Zack. Pete held him most of the days they were in the hospital. Mattie breastfed him and everything went smoothly. They took multiple pictures of each other and Zack. It was a happy time. Zack was beautiful!

Mattie wanted to name him Zachery Pete and call him Zack. Pete said then why not just name him Zack Pete Barton. (Some more of Pete's reasoning. LOL!) So that is what they named him. Zack was so sweet. He was a good baby and a joy to be around.

Pete was off work for a time to be with Mattie and Zack. He finally went back to work, and Mattie stayed home with Zack. I was off for several days and we enjoyed him so much. Mattie did not want me to hold him because she was afraid, he would think I was his mother. Well, I had to keep in mind that she was only 15 years old. LOL.

While we were there, Pete and Mattie both got their GED. Pete was able to take the test without studying, but Mattie had to study math and English. The school was Pitt Community College, and they were the first couple to graduate there, so they put it in the paper. I was so afraid someone from Louisiana would see the paper and come get Pete. That never happened. LOL. The guys' job ended in the fall of 1990, and we moved home. Pete, Mattie, and Zack decided to stay longer, but Mattie missed us, so they followed us home several days later.

It was very hard for me to leave my little girl. It is hard to see your children all grown. She will always be my little girl. Her personality was very outgoing, but her entire life was centered on their baby and Pete

CHAPTER EIGHT

We hired a lawyer to clear Pete's name and thought everything was okay. Pete had been cleared of his juvenile charges, but still had adult charges from the breakout in July. With all my stressors, I forgot the lawyer had told me not to let him come back to Louisiana; a pretty big thing to forget. LOL.

We were living at the farm and Bo was working at the paper mill in Bastrop, Louisiana. It was winter and deer season. Pete wanted to go hunting and drove our old truck to the back of our land to hunt early one Friday morning. Around ten a.m. he pulled to the front of the field and stopped for a car. It just happened to be the game warden and he stopped Pete. When they ran his name, they came up with a warrant for his arrest, so they took him to the Bastrop jail.

I was working in home health about 45 minutes away when I got a phone call telling me Pete had been arrested. I talked to someone who told me he had an outstanding warrant.

I said, "No! I have his papers with me. He is not wanted!"

The Game Warden told me, "He still has an outstanding warrant."

It was Friday afternoon by the time I got to the Bastrop jail. I found them and I told the warden,

"Let me contact his lawyer and get this straight."

He told me, "I've called LTI, and someone is coming to get him!

I was hysterical. Our lawyer was out of town, and I could not get anyone else to help us. About four p.m. we heard a man coming down the hall rattling chains. I was so upset, I was up in the warden's face, pushing him with my finger.

"You are just going to let them take him???" "I cannot believe this!"

He said, "MRS. STARKS, THERE IS NOTHING I CAN DO!"

I had told Pete one time if he was ever arrested, to be good because we were working to get him out. He took off his ring and handed it to me. I was crying and so scared.

We heard the guy from LTI coming down the hall, chains rattling as he came closer. This guy was solid, with large muscles. I thought I would faint. He said, "Someone at LTI wants you!"

He took Pete's hands and wrapped the chains around his hands, then ran the chain down to his feet and went about his ankles. Then he took Pete away. Pete was calm and serene.

All I could think is, "I need to talk to Bo. This is so wrong!"

I drove home and told Mattie what happened. Well, she became hysterical and started running.

She eventually calmed down and we talked about Bo coming home and helping us. Laney was also with us.

"What was happening???"

Later that afternoon, Mattie called LTI to find out about Pete. She told them she was his wife. They would not even acknowledge Pete was there. It was a very difficult time for Mattie, Laney, and me. We waited for Bo to get home, still no cell phones.

I met Bo as he drove up and told him what had happened. We tried to get information from the person at LTI, but she said she could not give out any information. She would not even say he was there. Bo listened and then said,

"I will call the Governor. He can find out."

We were so worried because Pete was too old to go to LTI. We did not know what they were doing with him. I had seen too much TV. LOL. Bo got the governor's aide. He explained what had happened and how LTI was responding to us. The governor's aide told him he would find out and call Bo back, so we sat close to the phone. When he called back, he said, "Mr. Starks, I think they'll talk to you now."

Bo called back and spoke with the dispatcher. He asked her if Pete was there and what they were doing with him. She told him he would be transferred to Baton Rouge Saturday and then she burst out crying and said, "I am just the dispatcher!" She had not believed the person on the phone was the governor's aide. He had finally told her, "If you do not give me some answers, I will have someone up there to investigate this situation tomorrow!"

We prayed so hard. Mattie paced and paced. As Saturday rolled around, Pete was transported on a white school bus. They gave him a set of clothes, which he was to wear for a month. They did not know what to do with him, so he just sat around. We were able to go see him on Sunday. We met in a large room with tables. We could bring him lunch, so we brought hamburgers. He looked great. Mattie was so much better after this. Thank God!

We finally got our lawyer and he got Pete out on a work release. We were so excited. Mattie, John, Mark, Bo, and I went back to Baton Rouge, a four-hour drive, and arrived about 5:00 p.m. Our car was a little Nissan hatchback, and it is a good thing there were no seat belt laws because we were a tight fit. LOL.

The grounds were beautiful, and they had a guard riding a big white horse over the grounds to watch for escapees. After a while, Pete and a guard came out. He was chained as before. They must have something about those chains. LOL. We were so happy to take him home even if his clothes smelled. LOL. Pete did not say much on the way home, but our kids never shut up. It was a happy time.

Our lawyer obtained a work release for Pete, so Monday morning, Pete and Bo went to work in Sterlington, Louisiana, for an industrial electrical construction company. After this job ended, we moved around to several other construction jobs and over the next four years, we took several jobs in the south and eventually moved to Utah to work in a copper mine.

While we were in Utah, Mattie and Laney were both pregnant. I was not working, and we had no insurance. Both girls decided to go back to Louisiana to have their babies in Bastrop. In June, Mattie had her second baby, a beautiful little girl. They named her Ginger. She was beautiful and has grown into a sweet young lady. In August, Laney had their first baby, a precious little boy. They named him Jason. He has become a sweet young man in a home with girls. LOL. It was a wonderful time for me. I rejoiced over my family and praised both girls for their beautiful deliveries.

CHAPTER NINE

Pete and Mattie talked nonstop with each other. Laney and I could not imagine what they could be talking about. They never shared. LOL. Pete never missed a day's work unless he asked off.

Time passed and we were working in Mississippi on a job at a plant. Bo and I, along with our families moved into a huge antebellum home in an old southern town and it was close to Christmas. When the job was completed, Bo contacted another supervisor who was working in New Mexico. Laney was pregnant with her second baby and was due December 14th. Laney went into labor and delivered on December 14th. It was a beautiful, baby girl, and they named her Jessie. Her hair was dark, and she was beautiful. She was a good baby.

The supervisor wanted us to come to New Mexico as soon as we could get there. That meant packing up, driving to Louisiana to visit my parents, and starting another adventure. We had an early Christmas and packed up to move. My sweet cat had died, and I told Bo I was not going to leave her in Mississippi, so we wrapped her up very tightly in a blanket and a black bag. Since it was cold, we laid her in the back of the truck. After we got to Louisiana, we drove to my grandparent's home and buried her there. I missed her, but I had not had her for long. I thought she was a young cat, but we decided later that she was quite old. She died in my lavatory, I tried to give her CPR, but she was already gone. I was home with Laney who was not fond of her, but she was supportive. I loved Callie.

After visiting with my parents and burying Callie, we headed out West. We were a little caravan. John had rented a U-Haul, Bo and I were in our truck with our things in the back, and Pete and Mattie had two vehicles. They packed in their four-runner. Mark stayed in Louisiana with his girlfriend.

When we got to Hurley, New Mexico, our supervisor was not there. Each of the guys rented a motel studio apartment about 15x15. It was very small. We settled in and looked around Hurley. It was so different from Louisiana. No trees, many cacti, and it was very cold. We were there one week before our supervisor showed up. He came in about 10 p.m. Friday and told us he had a surprising story.

He said, "Y'all are going to kill me, but I have taken a job in Casper, Wyoming, and we have to be there Monday morning. After the guys talked it over and since we were flexible, LOL, we packed up again, got our rent back, and headed to Wyoming.

Pete, being Pete, decided he would rather drive at night. There were still no cell phones and no way to keep track of Pete and Mattie. I was very unhappy, but Pete was insistent. That was a very trying night. It was snowing and the roads were mountainous and steep with drop-offs. The road was snowed over so it was hard to see. I did not sleep much. We arranged to call Pete's mother the next morning to check on Mattie. She said they safely arrived in Casper, Wyoming, and would meet us at Wal-Mart.

Pete's 4-runner had no heat and Zack rode with him. Mattie said she worried about him being cold. They drove 25 miles an hour and she was tense the entire way. She and Ginger were warm, and Ginger slept all the way. The next morning, bright and early, we pulled out of Hurley, New Mexico, and headed to Wyoming. The roads were frozen, with sludge from 18-wheelers on the road. When we got into Denver city limits, Bo was driving 60 miles an hour. He says, "I cannot see!" Then he rolls down his window and puts his head out the window, saying, "Hand me that bottle of water. I am going to throw it on the windshield to clear it."

I handed him the open bottle, he put his head out the window again and threw the water on the windshield. However, what made it to the windshield froze immediately, so his vision was worse. When he pulled his head back in, water had frozen all over his face: icicles on his hair, lips, and beard. He just looked at me. It was the funniest thing. I laughed and laughed and then said, "Yonder is a station! Pull in there! I Mean It! The reason he was trying to clear the windshield was that he did not want to stop. Believe it or not, he stopped. I never let him forget how stupid that was although I was scared to death, I kept my mouth shut. LOL. "NOT!"

We made it to Wal-Mart in Casper around ten and met Mattie and Pete. Boy, was I glad to see them. I am sure I have several gray hairs from that experience. LOL. When we got to a motel, the wind chill was -29 degrees. Our perishable items were all frozen and had to be thrown away. I had never seen frozen mayonnaise before. It was a memory for all of us. "WOW." The guys worked three weeks and were transferred to Guernsey, Wyoming.

We could not find anywhere to live so we drove to Fort Laramie. (not Laramie). There was a motel there. It was a very small town, maybe a village. It had a post office, a store/filling station, a restaurant, and a trading store on the main street very close to the road. The motel had four rooms and a shotgun house.

The kids along with mother moved into the rooms and Bo and I moved into the shotgun house. It was snowing and very pretty. Our place was directly across the road from an old church and a park. Birds were everywhere looking for food and water. How beautiful is God's creation? It was a postcard beautiful scenery and since we did not have phones or a camera, Zack and I only have that as a memory.

To the side of our house was a small place to run and play. Zack loved to go outside and play there. We were afraid to let him stay out too long since we were not sure about the weather. We could wear short sleeves later in the day, but it was still freezing. It was a dry cold, so it did not feel as cold as it was.

The guys had to work outside and hated it. By getting there at six a.m., they were in the brunt of the cold. Even though they dressed in layers, they were still cold. It snowed frequently and the wind blew all the time.

There was one public phone in front of the post office, just almost on the road. Mark had stayed in Bastrop at his girlfriend's home. They broke up and he wanted me to come get him.

I called to check on him and this was what I was met with…"Mama, I want you to come get me.

I said, "Mark, it is 1,100 miles and it is cold. Are you sure?"

"Yes, Mother! Come get me."

"OK! I am coming."

Minutes later, he would say, "Wait a minute. No, I will stay here." Then we would start over.

"Yes, Mother, come get me."

"Wait, Mother! Do not come yet. I will call you back tonight."

"Are you sure, Mark? I want to come get you."

"Yes, Mother, I am sure."

So, I would go stand in the freezing cold, next to the road with sludge being thrown on me by 18 wheelers passing, waiting for his call. This went on for several days, the same conversation. I finally told him he had to make up his mind because I was freezing while waiting to talk to him. I was almost worrying myself sick.

He finally told me he guessed he would stay. I made him promise to call me in a week after threatening him bodily harm if he did not call, then I would stand by the phone until it rang. I missed Mark very much and wanted him to be with us.

Since Zack had started kindergarten but was not going, I decided to homeschool him. He would come over to our house Monday through Thursday and do his paces. There was a window in front of his desk and as I said, a pretty old brick church was across the street with lots of birds around it. The snow completed the picture, and I would catch Zack just sitting there, watching the birds. I finally started pulling down the shade. Zack was always pleasant.

He liked it when we traveled to town. We went early and spent most of the day there. On the way home, a train always ran on tracks parallel to the road and Zack would watch it. It was about an hour one-way.

CHAPTER TEN

Zack is a very smart young man but has the strongest will I have ever seen. I would set the pages to complete each day. Some days it looked like he was working diligently but would have three or fewer pages done. It was frustrating. Other days he would finish 33 pages that I had assigned him.

Have you ever been in a blizzard? Well, we saw our first. It did not look too different because like I said, it snowed every day. Blizzards are a BIG deal. LOL. The gates on the north and south ends of town were closed and no one could leave. I was very concerned and talked to the lady at the filling station. She said not to worry. If she ran out of eggs, milk, and bread, she had some friends around on ranches that could bring us some. Good Grief!

The guys came home early from work, and we all rode around on the back roads looking at everything. It was about the same for us. In the south when it snows almost everything shuts down and we stay home. The definition of a blizzard is freezing snow blowing enough to stop traffic. It did not appear to be that bad.

After the guys went back to work the next day, they saw a snowdrift covering the road with hills on each side. It was pretty impressive, and Pete said, "I think I can drive through it with the 4-Runner." Bo and John said, "We think you can, too, so go for it!"

Pete backed up, got a running start, and drove straight into the snowdrift. The soft snow became a brick wall and completely covered the 4-Runner. They had to crawl out the windows and claw their way through the snow, then walk back to get another vehicle, laughing all the way.

It took two weeks before the 4-Runner could be seen. Since there was no traffic on this road, it was safe. When they went to work, they simply drove around the area. The snow finally melted enough to rescue the truck. It was an awesome experience for the guys.

Zack was always entertaining himself. Ginger was too little to play with, so he would go outside and play. As I said, there were so many birds. He discovered several birds lying "dead" on the ground. He picked them up and took them to the room in the motel. He collected quite a number of these birds and put them into the bathtub with the shower curtain pulled. That night when his mother got ready to bathe Zack, she pulled the curtain, and all the birds flew at her. It was quite exciting to Zack, but not so much to Mattie. LOL.

We stayed there three months and then went back to the farm. While we were home, Pete went to an instrumentation-electrician school that Bo graduated from in Baton Rouge, Louisiana. He stayed with Uncle Davis and Aunt Fanny in their upstairs studio apartment. He ate with them but did not talk much. LOL. That was Pete. They said they enjoyed having him there, that he was pleasant. We all loved Pete. Bo and the boys enjoyed working with him.

Pete went to school Monday through Friday in Baton Rouge, Louisiana, and came home on weekends. One day he called me and said,

"I've had a wreck."

I said, "Are you hurt?"

He said, "No, but the truck does not look too good."

I asked him about the other vehicle, and he said it was ok. He said he could drive home so I told him to come home. He worried all the way home and when he got there, I saw why. My heart almost stopped. The entire driver's side was crushed. He kept expecting to get stopped. That was a four-hour drive, but he made it. What can I say, Pete did not want to take time to get it fixed.

Pete graduated from LTI and moved back home. We hung out on the farm, a 108-acre farm outside Bastrop.

CHAPTER ELEVEN

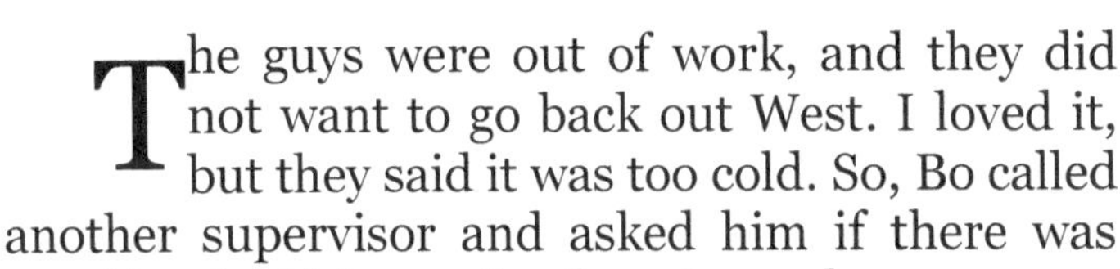

The guys were out of work, and they did not want to go back out West. I loved it, but they said it was too cold. So, Bo called another supervisor and asked him if there was anything in Alabama for them to work.

He said, "Yes, Come on," so we got the map down, looked up Decatur, Alabama, packed up, and headed to Decatur. I found a nice state park so I decided we could camp until we found somewhere to live. I did not know it was tornado season in northwest Alabama.

We drove into Decatur between two tornadoes, so we found a motel until we could find an apartment. Boy, it was the easiest place to rent yet. Thank you, Jesus!

Bo and I got a townhouse, and it was super. The girls were excited because we would be stationary for a while. It was a BIG job.

Well, the supervisor said, "Guys, you cannot start yet."

So, they waited. I applied for a job in Labor and Delivery at the small hospital there, to start work in July.

The guys waited and waited. Finally, Bo told the supervisor we were running out of money. He said, "Bo, this is a BIG job, they just keep putting me off."

Bo said, "Well, find us something else in TIC so we can work till it is ready. We will leave the families here." The supervisor found a job in Sugar Land, Texas, in Houston and they decided to go. My job did not start for several months but we decided to stay at the townhouse, and they left for Texas

Mark was now with us after staying with Mama until he finished school. Bo called another supervisor we knew, who was working in Baytown, and asked if they could stay with him until they got paid. The only problem with this was the hour-long drive to work in Houston.

During this time, Bo, John, Pete, and Mark all had a week's pay, but could not find anyone to cash their checks. The supervisor they were staying with was now letting them stay and feeding them, too.

Bo tried several places to cash the checks but to no avail. Finally, they mentioned it to several of the guys they were working with, and they told them there was a Quick Stop across the road from the plant that would cash them. They were so excited and so HUNGRY.

They decided to go to a seafood place to eat. They each ordered two entrees and when they finished, they moaned all the way back to the motel. Now when one of them says, "When were you the fullest?", they all say in Houston at the seafood place. This memory holds. LOL.

The guys finally found a studio apartment very close to the Sugar plant where they worked. (They all came back to Decatur saying they would never eat processed sugar again. We told them NOT to tell us why. LOL.) John, Pete, and Mark slept on the bed while Bo slept on the floor. He said that he had never slept with men and was not going to start now. LOL.

We all talked to the guys every night. Bo was cooking on the little stove, but Pete and Mark usually went out. There was a bar close by and they liked to go there and play pool. One night Pete called Mattie and was slurring his words. She thought he was drunk and proceeded to give him a lecture. Pete and Mattie had arguments over alcohol. It was an ongoing thing. Pete went long periods without drinking.

Anyway, Pete and Mark had gotten their tongues pierced. They were swollen, they could not talk right, and could not eat. Pete had wanted to surprise Mattie, but he finally told her what was wrong. LOL. It took about two weeks to get better. Later, Pete took his barbell out and Mark swallowed his. He called me at work and said, "Mother, I just swallowed my barbell." I had a flashback of a barbell for exercise. I started laughing. Finally, he made me understand and I told him we would just watch him for problems. I told him not to put another one in his tongue.

After a while, Mattie and Laney decided to go visit the guys so we packed up and headed to Houston, Texas. The guys got us a place to stay. We had a family meeting to discuss staying in Houston. Their job was good, and the guys wanted to stay. Laney and Mattie did not want to raise their children in Houston, so we all agreed to go back to Decatur until our supervisor was ready for start-up.

They had to build Worthington Steel from the ground up. After it was built, Worthington Steel hired Bo, Pete, John, and Mark. It was a big pay cut, but we now had stability, insurance, and other good benefits

CHAPTER TWELVE

Pete was a good worker. He enjoyed the work because he had a special way of looking at a problem. He would study for a while, then he would set out to fix it. It was not long until workers from all over the plant were calling him to solve and fix problems.

In April 1998, Mattie was pregnant with their third child. She had not planned to have any more children, but GOD told her she was going to have a little boy and to name him Noah. He was a precious little boy and when he was three weeks old, Mattie started school to be an RN. She started with one class, then would rush home and nurse Noah. She impressed me!

We found some land on Smith Lake and Bo and I bought a trailer and moved on the land. Soon, all three kids and families bought trailers and moved with us. Now we were driving 53 miles one-way to work. Mattie changed schools, continuing her education. It was an exciting day. Mother moved with us and bought a small trailer and moved it on our land. Pete and Mattie bought a double-wide trailer and a piece of land next to ours. John and Laney bought a trailer and moved onto our land.

Time passed. Bo and I found a home and land in Moulton and moved there. Mattie finished nursing school. She and Pete bought a home close by us in Moulton. It was a great home with lots of space. They put down an above-ground pool and we had lots of fun during the summer. Mattie was working as an RN in Decatur. Their home was always open to friends of their children. It was no surprise to see three or four guys sleeping crosswise on Noah's bed.

Pete liked to cook, so he would surprise Mattie with supper. He liked to try new recipes. Their favorite was a shrimp dish he cooked. When they asked Bo and me to eat with them, we always felt special. We tried to compliment Pete, but he would give that half-smile and say nothing.

He started growing a garden after he built Mamaw Tilbury an add-on to their home. She enjoyed getting vegetables from Pete's garden, especially purple hull peas. Pete ALWAYS wanted cornbread with his peas and mashed potatoes. Now, that was his favorite meal.

He would always be late for a holiday dinner. He would get there about the time we finished. He would walk into the kitchen and look at the dishes. If one of the three dishes were missing, he would say, "Where is the cornbread, or mashed potatoes?" (We always had peas). Mark's wife, Sarah makes a really good potato casserole, but Pete informed me it was not mashed potatoes.

(He liked Sarah's dish because he ate two or more helpings. LOL.)

Pete was a perfectionist. Bo went over to help him build the rooms onto his house for Mamaw, and he would come around and check on Bo's performance. Something was wrong with the vinyl Bo was putting up. Pete was fussing at Bo.

Bo said, "Pete! It is in the back. No one will see it." LOL. I never stayed to see if Pete changed it.

I think the funniest thing my grandchildren did was Noah sitting on the couch, watching the story of Noah and the ark. He was about four years old. He looks up at me and says, "Mamaw, I am that Noah!" then looks back at his show. I thought it was priceless.

When Zack was young, he had said the Pledge of Allegiance and at the end, he changed "with liberty and justice for all" to "with liver and Jesus for all." LOL. We made him say it over and over.

Children are so wonderful. Our grandchildren now numbered five. While they were in Moulton, Pete and Mattie started attending church at the Pentecostal Church in Moulton, Alabama. Mattie renewed her spiritual walk, and Pete was saved, baptized, and spoke in tongues. What a glorious time!

Pete and Mark were always close. They spent a great deal of time together and they hunted every season. Pete killed two deer and a bobcat and had them mounted. Mark killed two deer and a turkey and had them mounted.

Pete took Zack and Noah bow hunting. Zack said they rode four hours and "Daddy did not say a word." He also spent time with Ginger. He talked to her, helped her paint her room, and gave her money when she asked. He called her, "Daddy's little girl." He spent a lot of time with Mattie. They would have a "night out" quite frequently. Pete was a man of few words. He told you what he thought when you asked him. He would always come over when we needed some adjustment to our TV or DVD.

After seven or eight years, the steel plant sold most of their plant and offered jobs to all of them. Mark and Sarah (who were also working at the steel plant) accepted jobs from the new steel plant, and Bo and Pete stayed at their jobs.

John and his family had gone back to construction work because he was having a hard time financially. He now had four children. Two beautiful little girls were added, Callie and Leah. They moved to middle Alabama. We met them in Montgomery for special occasions. Once, we went to the mall and ice skated; that was fun. The steel plant downsized, and Pete was able to get on with the new steel plant. Bo stayed at his job.

One of the things they did not like about Pete was he did not talk. And when I say that, it is Pete. He continued to work in industrial/electrical maintenance at the new plant. He worked at the original steel plant for seven years, and the new steel plant for six years. He was sent to several places to learn something new. He never did say, but I think he enjoyed it. He partnered with several people during his time at work. They rode around in a tool cart. When they were called on a job, they usually had everything they needed.

His usual procedure was to get to a site, listen to the report of the problem, and walk around the site while smoking in one hand and drinking coffee in the other. Everyone learned to be quiet at this time LOL. Suddenly, he would say, "I think this is what is wrong." Then he would proceed to fix it. If someone disagreed with him, he would either look at them or just ignore them.

He did not realize it, but he was well-liked by everyone. I think it was because he was real, a good worker, and enjoyed people. What a change from the guy that would lean up against the wall waiting until time, then go to work. He slumped over, smoking, staying by himself. He had changed over the years. He was a good worker, a good husband, a good daddy, a good son-in-law, and a good friend.

CHAPTER THIRTEEN

In June 2013, Pete and Mattie planned a boat trip Saturday morning, and he had bought some new swimming trunks. He went to Mark's to get the boat and sat around talking to Mark and Sarah. She noticed he was a little nervous, but not enough to mention. He left there about 8:30 p.m. to go home. He had been fasting all week.

None of us know what happened to Pete. He bottled up his feelings. He had finally agreed to see a psychiatrist and had seen him Wednesday.

We do not know why he took his life. He had talked to Zack and told him he would always be there for him. He had tried once before with pills but lived. He told us next time he would not fail. I was working on six medicines for the bipolar syndrome, so I let it go. I want to say here, if someone you love tries to commit suicide, please seek help. Pete's visit to the psychiatrist did not trigger anything special Wednesday. I think Pete hid his feelings during the visit. He was on antidepressants. I had to pray for myself over this. Mattie and all three of his children have had a very difficult time not to mention Bo and me.

When Pete first came to live with us, he told me he was going to die at 29 yrs. old. Needless to say, I prayed about that. Eric told me later, Pete had always wanted to end his life as far back as 10 yrs. old. Our family was devastated, stunned with disbelief, and trying to make sense of it all. Looking from the outside, we could not understand why. I have learned to find the secret place to grow in FATHER'S LOVE.

It took me four years to stop going to his grave to talk to him. One day JESUS gave me a vision of Pete in heaven with Mamaw Tilbury. He loved her. It was peaceful. Thank YOU, JESUS.

At the funeral, several men from Pete's work spoke. One, in particular, stood out. He was a graduate and when they put him with Pete to partner, he thought how hard it would be trying to work with him. At first, he said he tried to tell Pete how to fix something. Eventually, he began to let Pete solve the problem. He said, "Pete would have a cup of coffee in one hand, and a cigarette in the other. He would walk around for a while looking at the problem site, studying it, and then Pete would say, 'It needs to be fixed like this," and sure enough, that fixed the problem.

He would say all the time, "What the Crap?"

I miss him.

When Pete answered the phone, he would say, "Yes?", and then wait. If you did not say anything, he would say, "Yes?" several times. It was hard to carry on a phone conversation with him. I think he enjoyed just being himself.

After being with us for several years, he learned to smile quite a lot. Especially if we caught him trying to joke with us, like the phone.

Looking back over the 22 years of his life with us, he was always a member of our family. All of us enjoyed spending time with him. He never talked about anyone. Pete went from a teenager with long hair and tattoos, to a responsible adult, a good husband, and dad.   He had a big piece of our hearts, and we miss him every day.

Will we see him again? Most Definitely!

Here's to Pete. We love you!

EPILOGUE

My friends asked me to write a postscript and after much thought, I agreed.

I intentionally did not talk about Zack's trouble with incarceration. His Mom and Dad spent many hours praying for him. And "God has done exceedingly, abundantly beyond anything we could ask or think!" Praise God. He is an awesome God!

Zack got out of prison on December 11th, 2017. I wanted to write Zack's story but there was so much we could not share about prison. I can say that it was GOD'S mercy that he was released. I can share this. FATHER GOD told me to start printing the report from the Department of Corrections stating when Zack would be released. As the time drew closer, I asked Zack if he wanted the copy of the report and he said, "Yes."

We talked all weekend and he said they never mentioned his release. He finally went to the office and told them he was going to be released Monday. They started laughing. He handed them the paper I had sent him and after reading it, they jumped up and started preparing for his release. I stand amazed at how loving JESUS IS.

Zack told us to be there at about 10 a.m. Monday. We were there and when he walked out, I was emotionally overcome. Mattie grabbed him and hugged him close. Then I hugged him, too. It was a wonderful day in my life. Today, Zack has started his own business and is happy. Thank YOU, JESUS.

After Pete was buried, Mattie grieved. We all did. The days in our home were quiet. Time stopped. I had trouble believing Pete was gone. Mattie wanted to die, too, but she realized she had three children that needed her. The following two years were hard for her, too.

She attempted to start a new life in Arkansas but to no avail. Ginger had gone with her, going to college, and Noah stayed with us and finished high school. He was outstanding at football, and he expected his mother to be at the games. She did not disappoint him

I went to the ladies' retreat from church that winter. While there, I was so touched by the Holy Spirit that I just prayed that Satan gave back all he had stolen from Pete's family. Then I asked my FATHER to send Mattie someone.

The following is a list of the things Satan stole from Pete, his family, and our family:

- Pete's Testimony
- His Family
- His Finances
- Pete's Prosperity
- His Worship

- His Calling
- Pete's Mind
- His Sanity
- His Relationships
- Pete's breach with The Starks

The following is a list of what Satan stole from Mattie:
- Her husband
- Mattie's companionship
- Mattie's Intimacy
- Mattie's Support
- Mattie's Best Friend

This is a list that I asked My FATHER for:
- A Godly son-in-law with a good job that fulfills every need in Mattie's life.
- Someone that will embrace her children and families. In Jesus' Name.

Well, Jesus did exceedingly abundantly beyond all that I could ask or think...." What a mighty GOD we serve! I Love you, JESUS. John and Jackie (John had gotten a divorce and married Jackie.) We now had four more grandchildren-two beautiful little girls and two handsome little boys. They were living at the farm, and John told Mattie,

"Mattie, why don't you call Eric's brother?"

Since Mattie was living in Arkansas, she was close to the farm and spent a lot of time with John and Jackie.

Mattie told John, "That feels weird, John, calling a man, even if he is Eric's brother." I think John got involved and played cupid. LOL.

Eric's brother came along and swept Mattie off her feet, giving her everything I had asked for her from our FATHER.

It was a good time for Mattie. Jim works construction as a welder. She has stayed in a camper most of their marriage. She has been happy but continues to cope with past guilt and sadness for her children. They have bought a house and land to live in when Jim retires. Mattie returned to work. We are so proud of her and love her very much.

Mark had Pete's R.I.P. date tattooed on his side. He talked to Bo about wondering if Pete went to heaven. Nowhere in the Bible does it say, "Believe in the Lord Jesus Christ and thou shalt be saved, except if you kill yourself." Or did Jesus say, "No one can pluck them out of my hand, except if you kill yourself."

After leaving the Pentecostal Church, God led us to a nondenominational church. The pastors are wonderful. During our journey there, Pastor spoke one Sunday on the subject of suicide. He said that if that person was a Christian, he or she was in heaven. Ginger was there that Sunday, and she said, "Mamaw, that makes me feel soooo much better."

Sarah has missed Pete because he came and worked on the crane she operates at work. He also came around to see how she was doing. She said, "I would catch myself looking for Pete."

Mark's daughter remembers the phone conversations with Pete, and smiles, "Hello, (long pause), Hello, Uncle Pete? (Long Pause). then he would finally start talking.

Bo is stoic concerning Pete. He is ever ready to defend him, even if it was something Pete did. We claim Pete as one of our children

THANK YOU LORD, FOR ALLOWING ME TO SHARE OUR LIVES WITH PETE. Through it all, I became closer and closer to JESUS. I linked up with a wonderful prayer partner and we began running after JESUS.

To my Readers, I say, "Be content. Live one day at a time. And trust in the Lord always and deepen your relationship with HIM, Look for your hiding place where JESUS meets with you. JESUS loves you so, so much and HE IS COMING BACK!"

MY THOUGHTS ON SUICIDE

Suicide is the most devastating issue because it is final. It is impossible to escape the horror of it. There is nowhere to run.

Guilt comes first. "If I had only done this or that." "I think I could have stopped him/her if I had only tried."

Pete and Mattie were angry with me, so I did not talk to him. The doctor would not let Mattie call Pete. She was discharged from the hospital but was not feeling good. After she got home, she laid down.

Pete visited with Mark and Sarah but did not discuss anything about taking his life. They talked about using the boat on Saturday. Ginger passed him sitting in his truck when she got home, which she thought was strange, but did not stop to talk to him.

Noah was not home, and Zack was in prison. Around 10 p.m. Mattie woke and started looking for him. She and a friend went to our place on Smith Lake, but he was not there. Pete was at Bankhead Forest where he hunted. He smoked for about 45 minutes. Several teenagers found him later and called 911.

Bo and I sat at home, stunned and unable to move. There was such an overwhelming sense of loss and emptiness. When Mark got home from work, we drove to Bankhead. As the family found out, we were speechless. Some of us cried. Some of us stared off into space. We could not sleep. We just sat without talking. Time stopped.

Saturday, Bo and Mattie went to the funeral home to make arrangements. Ginger picked out his shirt. We were not hungry, so no one ate lunch. The funeral was very good. The men that he worked with came and several spoke. Bo led the service.

We were given a book by our pastors, Pastor Tony and Ms. Sonya, entitled "Life After Death" by Tony Cooke. I tried to read it but finally laid it down. I could not keep my mind on it. The book described how we felt. We felt disorganized, disoriented, and unable to plan even the smallest tasks. Shock is a common experience in dealing with loss.

As Christians, we understand our GOD is with us. HIS LOVE for us and HIS desire to comfort us is consistent. We talked with HIM. I would close my eyes and ask HIM to hold me. It was a hard time for Bo and me because Pete had been with us 22 years and we felt like he was a son. He was special to us. How were we going to get along without him?

I later read some of the books I mentioned previously. It pointed out that grief is a process that we go through; shock, disbelief, anger, sadness, tears, and feeling out of control. Each person experiences these and time is not a factor. It never completely goes away but gets easier. I described my feelings like a motorboat passing by you. At first, the waves are strong and high. Then they get smaller and smaller. Finally, they are just ripples.

I conclude that what has been in your head, is now in your heart. You are coping. It has been six years and I have peace, knowing Pete is in heaven. People will want to put their beliefs on you about where Pete might be. I asked GOD to protect me from people's opinions and HE did. I am at peace with HOLY SPIRIT.

Pete was a Christian. I want to encourage anyone going through this crisis to know that if your loved one accepted JESUS, HE made a way for them. Another thing I strongly recommend is to find a support group or psychologist and share with them. We all would have benefited from help. Please talk to someone that will listen if you are having suicidal thoughts.

JESUS LOVES YOU.

"When peace like a river attendeth my soul. When sorrows like sea billows roll. Whatever my lot THOU hast taught me to say, 'IT IS WELL, IT IS WELL WITH MY SOUL.'" by Horatio Spafford

and composed by Philip Bliss. First published in
GOSPEL HYMNS NO. 2 by Ira Sankey and Bliss.
(1876)

TESTIMONIES ON SUICIDE

Grace's Testimony

Hello, my name is Grace, and this is my story about overcoming mental health, depression, and death. From December 22, 2013, until March 2014, I struggled with depression. At this time, I began cutting myself to relieve the deep sadness I felt. My parents took me to the clinic and after talking with a therapist, I was taken to Birmingham. Since I was only 13 years old, they had to pull me off my Dad. I could not understand why I could not stay with my parents.

This is when it all began and continued until 2020. I was hospitalized in every facility, and I was abused...verbally, sexually, and physically. I tried to report it the first time, but they did not believe me and put me on very strong medication. I was like a zombie. During this five-day stay, my parents slept in the car. Because I was crying, they would not let me eat. On the fifth day after being with me, my Dad took me out against medical advice. He said there was something wrong with me. This was in March 2014.

In April 2014, I went to the bathroom at school and made myself vomit. I was always bullied in school from fourth grade through ninth grade. I just could not take it anymore. The school counselor came and helped me to her office.

She called my parents to come get me and take me to the emergency room. From there I was transferred to a mental health facility for a week. When I got out of that place, I started going to a clinic in Cullman.

Between the years 2014-2016, this therapist sent me to the children's hospital five times. I could not understand why my body "felt so bad." I was going through a lot mentally and physically. After trying to report the first abuse, I did not tell anyone else. My suffering was mine alone. I could not get away from it. In January 2016, I was hospitalized from the twenty-sixth for six days and transferred to another facility for eight days. Then I was transferred to another place for six days, then another transfer for 35 days.

After this period, I was sent to a long-term facility. They could not decide what to do with me. I slept continuously, without going to shower or eat. So, at 15 years old, I was given one of the strongest medications for an adult. I took it twice a day. I was sexually abused during this time. There was no resistance in me. When my parents sat down with the psychiatrist, they told him I was eating my mashed potatoes with my fingers. I did not realize I was in the world. The psychiatrist said, "Well, at least she is not hurting herself." They replied, "Well, heck, she can't do anything. Y'all got her knocked out of her mind."

I got out of this horrible pickle on December 15, 2016, and got off that medicine. I still couldn't escape my thoughts of all I had gone through at the facilities, so I went and bought several blades. I didn't know any other way to release my emotions of what the male staff had done to me.

I cut my arms pretty bad. My dad took me to my appointment with the therapist. When she saw the blood on my shirt, she asked to see my arms. I didn't want to show her, but I finally did. She immediately got me admitted to one of the facilities I had already been in. This time, they ran all over me, calling me names, claiming I did things that I didn't do. They were verbally, physically, and sexually abusive.

When I tried to talk about Jesus, they put me on more medicines. When I left, I was on 23 different medications. I finally had to go back to the only facility I felt loved at because I had run from my house up the road and laid down at the bottom of a hill hoping to get run over. A man who knew my dad helped me to his truck and took me home.

Boy, did that truck feel good with the air conditioner running on this July 5, 2018. This time I also had to go through court to be placed because I had been hospitalized 14 times. They put me on suicide watch. Someone had tried to harm themselves with a zipper, so they took my clothes and put me in a gown and housecoat without personal clothes. The abuse continued. I was discharged home on July 6, 2020. I was raised in church enjoying Vacation Bible School and Gospel Singings. Most of the facilities would not let me talk about church and Jesus. But I would not be here if it was not for the Blood of Jesus Christ.

During this time, I became an aunt. I was so excited, and I wanted to see him. I had given my life to the Lord and turned my life over to Him on November 29, 2020. My friend took me to a brush arbor service and after the preacher brought the message about how he finally got the courage to be saved and shook off his chains and shackles, I wanted what he had gotten. I wanted to go to the altar every night.

I finally got the courage and asked my brother to go with me. I was crying and I said, "Can you pray for me?" He said "Yes," and started crying too. I would start to go down then back up. Finally, I made it down the front. The church was over and they were cleaning. I poured all my problems on Jesus for that is what He wants. Several men and women came and laid hands on me and prayed for me. I came up from that altar a different person. I felt amazing!

On March 22, 2021, I went to a revival at New Beginnings Church. Jesus loves you. He is so amazing So many times, people told me I would not make it in life. I was told I would be institutionalized in a mental hospital, never get my high school diploma, get my license, or live by myself in my own home. I got my diploma on May 22, 2021, my license on May 19, 2021, and finished my house on November 5, 2021. I moved into my home all because of Jesus Christ our Lord.

If Jesus can save my soul, He can do it for you, also. *Jesus is the same yesterday, today, and forever.* Hebrews 13: 8.

Jesus is waiting on us. I want to say that depression, suicide, drugs, and self-harm do not have control over you, you have control over them. I am a new person after finding Jesus. I claim victory and healing over your life like I did my own. I am a suicide survivor of 25 attempts to harm myself; over-dose, cut my body, swallowing marker tops, pencils, erasers, paper, crayons, tweezers, cat claws – I pushed their claws out and tried to scratch me/bite me. I now have scars on my whole body that show how Jesus healed me by His stripes.

Mental Health is so hard. I have Post Traumatic Syndrome Disorder (PTSD) from all the trauma I have been through since being in so many hospitals and being abused for years. I try not to let that bother me. My nephew did not know his Aunt Grace for three and a half years. I wanted to live for him and myself and with Jesus' help, I can.

I love you all. Tell your story. Do not be ashamed. Call on Jesus. He will hear and listen because Jesus has a purpose for us all. I'm still alive because of Him. Thank You, Jesus.

Faith's Testimony

My name is Faith, and this is my story. When I was 11 years old, I do not know how it started. I have always been to myself, I guess, and I started pulling away from my family and friends. I got to staying in my room and not being social. I guess it started then. I felt myself withdraw.

My Mamaw asked me if I was alright. She reached out to me, so I told her. She said to tell someone. I love my parents, but I knew they would rush me to a doctor or clinic, and I did not want to go.

I decided to tell my sister. We talked and she wanted me to talk to her boyfriend's sister. She had thoughts, too. We went to her house and talked with her. When I got back home, I said, 'Ok, it finally clicked. This is really bad. It is out there. I have got to get it together. It is out there, and I have got to get it settled, so calm down.' The friend helped me a lot. I think her mother took her to the doctor and she got on medicine. I did not want medicine.

I started going to a smaller church and began to take part in a lot of activities. That helped me

very much. I finally told my parents and they talked with me and helped me focus on Jesus. I would say to someone thinking about suicide, please go ahead and talk to someone. There are a lot better ways to release those feelings, and I am glad I am alive today. I am happy at 17 years old. I still have problems, but I know Jesus helps me.
JESUS LOVES YOU!

Patience's Testimony

My name is Patience, and this is my story. I was probably 11 years old. I had known about it. It was on my phone. That is where I learned a lot about it on my phone on the internet.

When I was really little, I had seen cuts on my cousin's arm, and I did not know what it was. She said that she was trying to hurt herself and I knew it must be bad. I knew she was unhappy. Later, I would get on my phone and see pictures of people cutting themselves and using razors. Once I started looking at it, I just kept pulling it up. I guessed if you were sad, that is what you did to your arm. In my head, it was like a math equation. If this and this, then this is the solution. Which is sad really.

I had thoughts about it a lot even before Pete killed himself and I want to say I was 13 or 14 years old. My sister saw my arm and she knew. She turned and looked at me and I knew. After dinner, on the way home, we talked about it. It helped that my sister knew, and I thought about how I would feel if one of my sisters did it. Who would find me? I didn't want to tell my mom because I knew how she would react. She would blame herself. She would worry and I did not want that. Mom would think she failed me.

For about two years I thought about it. I think it is like drugs. Late at night when everyone was asleep, I would go into the bathroom and cut my arms. It would make me feel better. I would clean the bathroom and do ok until the pressure got worse, and I would do it again. I began to shoplift gauze and Band-Aids so Mom would not find out. If Mom found a supply of gauze and Band-Aids, she would question me. It is so loud in your head you have to do something. I relate it to how a drug addict reacts.

I wanted help. I wanted to escape. You are valuable. You are important. You think it is imminent, but it is not. I got over it. It got better, but it started coming back. I think it is a spirit. I went to my stepdad, and he prayed with me. I think it was when I gave myself completely to Jesus that I was free. I just turned everything over to Him. I am glad I am alive. I have a wonderful job and just bought a new car. I still have issues, but Jesus cares and takes care of me.

He will help you too. Reach out. Use the hotline numbers. These people care. They are not out there for show. Use the real numbers you can call. Family cares, friends care, Jesus cares. Go buy a Bible. I know people are going to walk out of this if they will just talk to someone and keep sharing until someone takes them seriously. JESUS LOVES YOU!

Linda's Testimony

The effectual fervent prayer of a righteous man availeth much. James 5: 16

While living in a small town in Texas, my granddaughter and I were in a small church, and you could feel God's presence. I had been coming against the principality of suicide in prayer. I had prayed and fasted for quite some time.

Pete's daughter was telling this lady about her dad. This lady began to tell her about what all God had done for her and simply said, "My first husband committed suicide and when she said that, Holy Spirit said, "...and they overcame by the word of his testimony." I knew He had answered my prayers. I rejoiced greatly. He's such a personal GOD. HE IS LOVE!

I hope these testimonies have helped you understand that if you are thinking thoughts of harming yourself, please do not carry it out. There is so much to live for. The important thing is, suicide is not a choice, it is final. You are special. Jesus thought you are special enough to die for. YES, YOU! Live for yourself! Live for Jesus!

ABOUT THE AUTHOR

Linda Starks is a retired RN who worked in Labor and Delivery for 36 years. During her time in the Labor and Delivery room, she learned compassion and patience for people who have served her throughout her life. She counted it a joy to serve the people God brought across her path.

Linda and her husband, Bo, make their home in Moulton, Alabama. Since retiring, they both enjoy traveling for pleasure and meeting new people along the way with whom they can share the love of God.

They are originally from Louisiana and have three grown children. They have 16 grandchildren, five great-grandchildren.

ABOUT THE BOOK

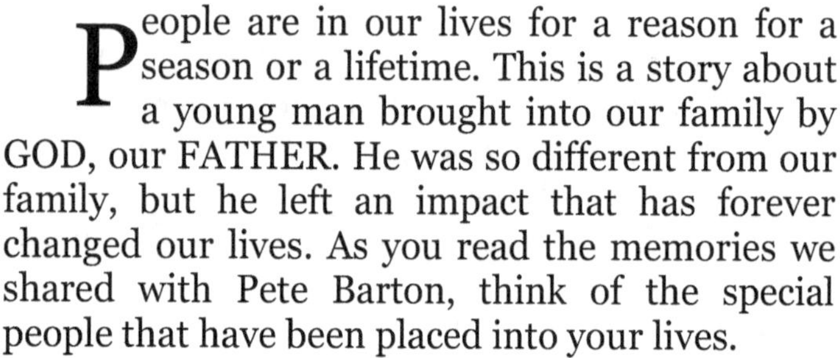

People are in our lives for a reason for a season or a lifetime. This is a story about a young man brought into our family by GOD, our FATHER. He was so different from our family, but he left an impact that has forever changed our lives. As you read the memories we shared with Pete Barton, think of the special people that have been placed into your lives.

Remember one small kindness can make the people and our world a better place. Battling depression is part of many people's lives every day. Some find that suicide is the only way out for the hopelessness that strikes full force. If you are thinking about suicide or know someone that keeps bringing it out in a conversation,

PLEASE talk to someone that will listen and help. Be relentless. It is worth it. I wish I had talked with him after the first failed attempt. Remember, regret is part of the grieving process. Thank you for reading my book,

Linda Starks

9 798885 266277